Mastering TikTok S̲_____: ___
Ultimate Guide to Viral Success

Introduction

The Rise of TikTok: Why Short Videos Dominate Social Media

In the fast-paced digital age, attention spans are shrinking, and content consumption has evolved. TikTok has emerged as a cultural phenomenon, captivating millions with its short, engaging videos. From dance challenges to life hacks, the platform has revolutionized the way we share and consume information, solidifying its place as the dominant force in social media.

Understanding TikTok's Potential: Entertainment, Education, and Business

Beyond the fun and entertainment, TikTok offers a unique blend of creativity and opportunity. It serves as a hub for educational content, connecting learners and teachers globally, and a powerful marketing tool for businesses of all sizes. By tapping into its potential, creators and entrepreneurs can build communities, share knowledge, and grow their brands.

Purpose of This Guide: Helping You Create, Grow, and Thrive

Whether you're new to TikTok or looking to refine your strategy, this guide is your roadmap. From creating captivating content to building a loyal following, we'll explore the tools, techniques, and trends that drive success. Together, we'll unlock the secrets to thriving in the ever-evolving world of short-form videos.

IDEA1: Understanding TikTok's Algorithm

How the Algorithm Works: The "For You" Page (FYP) Mechanics

At the heart of TikTok's success is its sophisticated algorithm, which powers the "For You" page (FYP)—a personalized feed tailored to each user's interests. This algorithm analyzes user behavior, such as video interactions, profile visits, and content preferences, to curate a seamless, engaging experience. Understanding how this system operates is the first step toward mastering the platform.

Key Factors: Watch Time, Engagement, and Consistency

TikTok's algorithm prioritizes content based on three main factors:

- **Watch Time**: Videos with higher average watch durations signal value to the algorithm, boosting their visibility.

- **Engagement**: Likes, comments, shares, and saves indicate audience interest and drive further reach.
- **Consistency**: Regular posting and maintaining a niche help the algorithm identify and promote your content to relevant audiences.

Decoding Trends: How to Identify and Leverage Them

TikTok thrives on trends, often sparked by music, hashtags, or challenges. Staying ahead means:

- **Monitoring the FYP**: Spot emerging patterns and viral content in real-time.
- **Using Trending Sounds and Hashtags**: Incorporating popular elements increases the likelihood of your video reaching a wider audience.
- **Creating Trend-Inspired Content**: Add your unique spin to trends to stand out while staying relevant.

By understanding and leveraging TikTok's algorithm, you can amplify your content's reach and make your mark in the dynamic world of short-form video creation.

IDEA2: Setting the Foundation

Defining Your Niche and Audience

Success on TikTok begins with clarity.

- **Identify Your Niche**: Determine the themes or topics that align with your passion, expertise, and what resonates with your target audience. Popular niches include fitness, education, lifestyle, comedy, and DIY projects.
- **Understand Your Audience**: Who are you speaking to? Analyze your ideal audience's age, interests, and challenges to create content that connects and delivers value. By honing in on your niche and audience, you'll set the stage for consistent and engaging content creation.

Creating an Optimized TikTok Profile

Your profile is your digital storefront—it's the first impression users have of you. Ensure it's inviting and professional:

- **Username**: Choose a username that is easy to remember, reflects your niche, and aligns with your brand identity.
- **Bio**: Use concise, compelling language to describe who you are, what you offer, and why users should follow you. A call-to-action (CTA), such as "Follow for daily tips!" can boost engagement.
- **Links**: Utilize TikTok's bio link to direct followers to other platforms, websites, or resources. If eligible, link your Instagram or YouTube accounts to expand your reach.

Tools and Apps for Video Editing

High-quality videos stand out on TikTok. While the platform offers built-in editing features, external tools can elevate your content:

- **Editing Apps**: Use apps like CapCut, InShot, or Adobe Premiere Rush to add professional-grade effects, transitions, and overlays.
- **Graphics and Animations**: Canva or Mojo can help you design eye-catching intros, outros, or on-screen text.
- **Music and Sound Effects**: Explore royalty-free sound libraries or TikTok's own library to find the perfect audio to complement your videos.

By defining your niche, optimizing your profile, and utilizing the right tools, you'll build a strong foundation for growth and engagement on TikTok.

IDEA3: Crafting Irresistible Content

The Anatomy of a Viral TikTok Video: Hook, Story, and CTA

Every viral TikTok video has a compelling structure:

- **Hook (0–3 seconds)**: Capture attention immediately. Start with an intriguing question, unexpected action, or visually striking element to stop viewers from scrolling.

- **Story (5–15 seconds)**: Deliver engaging content with a clear beginning, middle, and end. Whether it's a tutorial, skit, or behind-the-scenes moment, aim for authenticity and clarity.
- **Call-to-Action (CTA)**: Encourage interaction with simple prompts like "Follow for more tips," "Comment your thoughts," or "Share if this helped you." Effective CTAs increase engagement and drive audience growth.

Creating Authentic and Relatable Content

Authenticity is TikTok's currency. Users gravitate toward creators who are genuine and relatable:

- **Show Personality**: Share personal stories, behind-the-scenes moments, or raw emotions to build a connection with your audience.
- **Engage in Trends**: Participate in trending challenges or memes, but add your unique twist to maintain authenticity.
- **Solve Problems or Entertain**: Think about what your audience needs—be it a quick laugh, practical advice, or inspiration—and deliver accordingly.

Leveraging Music, Effects, and Transitions Effectively

TikTok is a platform driven by creativity and visuals. Enhance your content with these elements:

- **Music**: Choose trending or genre-appropriate tracks from TikTok's library to align with your content's vibe.
- **Effects**: Use TikTok's filters, slow-motion, and augmented reality (AR) features to add polish and excitement.
- **Transitions**: Smooth and clever transitions between clips keep viewers engaged and elevate your production value. Apps like CapCut can help create seamless transitions.

Dos and Don'ts for TikTok Shorts

Dos:

- Be consistent with your niche.
- Use high-quality lighting and audio.
- Engage with comments and build a community.
- Experiment with different video formats and analyze what works.

Don'ts:

- Avoid overly scripted or forced content.
- Refrain from using copyrighted music or unlicensed materials.
- Don't post inconsistently; the algorithm rewards regular activity.

- Don't overuse hashtags—focus on a few relevant ones.

By mastering these techniques, you can craft videos that resonate with audiences, encourage interaction, and have the potential to go viral.

IDEA4: Engaging with Your Audience

The Importance of Comments and Interactions

Audience engagement is the lifeblood of TikTok success. Actively interacting with your viewers can foster loyalty and amplify your reach:

- **Reply to Comments**: Respond to questions, thank users for their feedback, or simply react to humorous comments. This builds a sense of connection.
- **Pin Top Comments**: Highlight insightful or funny comments to encourage further interaction.
- **Ask for Feedback**: Use your comments section as a way to understand your audience's preferences and improve future content.

Using Duets and Stitches to Grow Your Reach

TikTok's unique duet and stitch features are powerful tools for engagement and collaboration:

- **Duets**: Share your screen with another creator's video. Use this to react, complement, or add value to existing content.
- **Stitches**: Incorporate a short segment of another video into your own, creating a seamless connection between the two. This is perfect for responding to prompts, challenges, or trending content. By leveraging these features, you can tap into larger audiences and demonstrate your creativity while aligning with trending themes.

Building a Community Through Live Sessions and Q&As

Live interactions take engagement to the next level by creating real-time connections:

- **Host Live Sessions**: Share updates, answer questions, or simply chat with your audience. Live sessions create an intimate and interactive experience.
- **Conduct Q&As**: Use TikTok's Q&A feature to invite specific questions from your audience. Answering these questions on live or in dedicated videos fosters trust and shows that you value your community's input.
- **Collaborate in Live Rooms**: Join other creators in live streams to cross-pollinate audiences and expand your reach.

By prioritizing engagement, you'll not only grow your following but also cultivate a loyal community that actively supports your content.

IDEA5: Trends, Hashtags, and Challenges

Spotting Trends Early and Riding the Wave

TikTok thrives on trends that can propel creators into viral territory. To stay ahead:

- **Monitor the FYP**: Spend time on the "For You" page daily to identify recurring themes, sounds, or video formats.
- **Follow Influencers**: Keep an eye on key creators in your niche—they often set or popularize trends.
- **Use TikTok's Discover Page**: This feature highlights trending hashtags and challenges, helping you spot opportunities early.
  By acting quickly, you can align your content with emerging trends, boosting its relevance and visibility.

The Power of Challenges: Starting and Joining

Challenges are the lifeblood of TikTok's interactive culture:

- **Joining Challenges**: Participate in popular challenges to tap into their pre-existing momentum. Add your personal twist to stand out while staying true to the challenge's core theme.

- **Starting Your Own Challenge**: Create a unique, shareable concept that aligns with your brand. Use a catchy hashtag and clear instructions to encourage participation. Partnering with influencers can amplify its reach.

Challenges not only increase engagement but also position you as a trendsetter within the TikTok community.

Effective Use of Hashtags for Discoverability

Hashtags are essential for categorizing and discovering content on TikTok. To maximize their impact:

- **Use Trending Hashtags**: Incorporate hashtags relevant to current trends, but ensure they align with your content.
- **Mix Popular and Niche Hashtags**: Combine widely used hashtags (#fyp, #trending) with niche-specific ones to target both broad and specific audiences.
- **Create a Branded Hashtag**: Develop a unique hashtag for your content or challenges to build brand recognition and encourage user-generated content.

Avoid overloading your videos with hashtags. Instead, focus on a strategic mix of 3–5 relevant and impactful tags to boost your content's discoverability.

By mastering trends, challenges, and hashtags, you'll position your content for maximum visibility and engagement on TikTok.

IDEA6: Monetizing Your TikTok Presence

Joining the TikTok Creator Fund

The TikTok Creator Fund offers an opportunity for creators to earn money based on the performance of their videos. To join:

- **Eligibility**: You must have at least 10,000 followers, 100,000 video views in the last 30 days, and be 18 years or older.
- **Application Process**: Once you meet the requirements, apply through your TikTok settings.
- **Earnings**: Payments are based on factors such as video views, engagement, and the authenticity of your content. The more you post and engage with your audience, the more potential earnings you have. Joining the Creator Fund allows you to start earning passive income from the content you create, but keep in mind that the pay varies depending on video performance.

Collaborations and Sponsorships

Once you've built a solid following and established your niche, collaborations and sponsorships can become a major revenue stream:

- **Brand Partnerships**: Brands are often looking to partner with TikTok creators to promote products or services. The key is to align with brands that resonate with your audience.
- **Sponsored Content**: Post sponsored videos that integrate a product or message naturally. Transparency is essential—always disclose sponsored content to maintain trust with your audience.
- **Affiliate Marketing**: Promote products through affiliate links. You earn a commission every time someone makes a purchase through your link.
- **Collaborating with Other Creators**: Teaming up with other influencers can expand your reach and open doors for joint sponsorships or cross-promotion opportunities.

Both collaborations and sponsorships allow you to leverage your growing influence while ensuring that your content remains authentic to your followers.

By exploring these monetization strategies, you can turn your TikTok presence into a profitable venture.

Selling Products or Services Through TikTok

TikTok provides several features to help creators sell products or services directly to their audience:

- **TikTok Shop**: The TikTok Shop allows creators to sell products directly from their profile or in video descriptions. To use it, you need to apply for access to the platform's shopping feature and link your store.
- **Affiliate Marketing**: Share affiliate links to products or services that you believe will resonate with your audience. Every time someone makes a purchase through your link, you earn a commission. Use engaging videos to showcase how the products work in your everyday life.
- **Linking to Your Website or E-Commerce Store**: If you have an online store (e.g., through Shopify or Etsy), you can include links in your bio or within video descriptions to drive traffic and encourage purchases.
- **Product Promotion**: Whether it's your own merchandise, an online course, or a subscription-based service, TikTok's video format makes it easy to engage your audience and drive interest in your products. Use video storytelling to showcase the value and benefits, and consider offering exclusive discounts or promotions to TikTok followers.

Selling through TikTok requires balancing your content strategy with authentic product promotion. Focus on delivering value while integrating your products or services naturally into your videos.

Driving Traffic to Other Platforms

TikTok isn't just about building a community within the app—it's also a tool to drive traffic to your other platforms or business ventures:

- **Linking to External Websites**: TikTok allows you to add a clickable link to your bio (for accounts with over 1,000 followers). This is a great way to direct traffic to your blog, e-commerce store, or other social platforms like Instagram, YouTube, or your personal website.
- **Cross-Promoting on Other Platforms**: Use TikTok to drive traffic to your Instagram, YouTube, or Twitter accounts. For example, create teaser videos that promote longer-form content on YouTube or share exclusive content on Instagram that complements your TikTok presence.
- **Email List Building**: Encourage viewers to sign up for your email list by offering downloadable content, exclusive updates, or discounts. Include a link in your bio or use your videos to promote sign-ups.
- **Live Sessions with External Links**: In TikTok live sessions, you can promote your website, products, or services. Engage with your audience in real-time while subtly

mentioning your other platforms or offerings, always with a clear CTA to visit those links.

By strategically leveraging TikTok as a traffic-driving tool, you can expand your reach and funnel followers to your other ventures, ultimately increasing your online presence and profitability.

IDEA7: Analytics and Growth Strategies

Understanding TikTok Analytics: Metrics That Matter

To optimize your TikTok strategy and fuel growth, you need to leverage TikTok's built-in analytics. These key metrics provide insight into how well your content is performing:

- **Video Views**: Track the number of views your videos are getting. This indicates the overall reach of your content and helps you understand what resonates with your audience.
- **Engagement Rate**: Engagement includes likes, comments, shares, and saves. This metric is crucial for understanding how much your audience is interacting with your videos. A high engagement rate suggests that your content is compelling.
- **Follower Growth**: This shows how your followers are growing over time. Pay

attention to spikes in growth after specific videos or campaigns.

- **Watch Time**: This is one of the most critical metrics. The more time people spend watching your videos, the more likely TikTok's algorithm will promote them to others.
- **Audience Demographics**: TikTok provides insights into your followers' age, gender, location, and activity times. This helps you tailor your content to better suit your target audience.
- **Traffic Sources**: This shows where your views are coming from, whether from the FYP, your profile, or direct links. Understanding traffic sources allows you to optimize your content for specific channels.

These metrics give you an actionable overview of your content's performance. By analyzing them regularly, you can identify trends and make data-driven decisions to improve your strategy.

Iterating Based on Performance Data

Growth on TikTok is a continual process of testing, learning, and adapting. Here's how to iterate based on your performance data:

- **Content Adjustments**: If certain videos are performing well, analyze what worked (topic, format, timing, etc.) and replicate those elements. For videos that don't perform well, consider experimenting with different approaches.

- **Optimize Posting Times**: Use the insights on audience activity to post at times when your audience is most active. Posting at the right time increases the likelihood of your video appearing on the FYP.
- **Content Type and Length**: Test various video formats (e.g., tutorial, behind-the-scenes, skits) and video lengths. If short-form videos perform better than longer ones, adjust your content accordingly.
- **Hashtag Strategy**: Evaluate which hashtags are generating the most engagement and refine your hashtag strategy based on performance. You may need to switch from overly popular hashtags to more niche ones that better match your audience.
- **Collaborations and Trends**: Track the success of collaborations or trends you've participated in. If certain partnerships or challenges yield higher engagement, prioritize them in future content creation.

Analytics allow you to track your progress and make informed decisions about future content and growth strategies. The more data you analyze, the better you'll understand your audience and how to serve them, fueling your growth on TikTok.

Scaling Up: Paid Promotions and Cross-Platform Strategies

Once you've built a solid presence on TikTok and refined your content strategy based on analytics, it's time to scale your growth. This can be achieved through paid promotions and cross-platform strategies. Here's how:

Paid Promotions

Paid promotions can rapidly increase your reach, boost engagement, and help you grow your audience quickly. TikTok offers several paid promotion tools that can be leveraged for maximum impact:

- **TikTok Ads**: TikTok provides multiple ad formats, including In-Feed ads, Branded Hashtag Challenges, and TopView ads (which appear when users first open the app). These ads allow you to target specific demographics and interests, giving you a broader reach.
    - o **In-Feed Ads**: These ads appear in users' For You page feed, much like regular TikTok videos. You can create engaging content with a strong call-to-action (CTA) to drive traffic or conversions.
    - o **Branded Hashtag Challenges**: Sponsor a challenge to get more users involved and create user-generated content that promotes your brand. This increases visibility and

interaction while engaging the TikTok community.

- ○ **TopView Ads**: These appear at the very top of the For You page when users open the app. They are more prominent and can result in higher engagement.
- **Targeting**: TikTok Ads Manager allows for precise targeting based on factors like location, interests, behaviors, and demographics. Use this feature to ensure your ads are reaching the right audience.
- **Budgeting and Bidding**: Set a budget for your campaigns and choose between automatic or manual bidding options. Start with a smaller budget to test the performance of your ads and scale up as you find what works best.

Cross-Platform Strategies

Expanding your reach beyond TikTok to other platforms helps you connect with a wider audience and cross-promote your content. Here's how to make cross-platform strategies work for you:

- **Repurpose Content**: Use TikTok videos to fuel your content on other platforms. For example, post your TikTok videos on Instagram Reels, YouTube Shorts, or Twitter. Each platform has its own audience, so adapting your content can help attract new followers.

- o **Instagram**: Share TikTok videos directly to your Instagram feed or stories. Use Instagram's features like polls, quizzes, and questions to drive engagement.
- o **YouTube**: Post a compilation of your best TikTok videos as long-form content. You can also create reaction videos or "TikTok compilations" that drive traffic to your TikTok profile.
- o **Facebook and Twitter**: Share your TikTok content to these platforms to reach different demographics and bring more people to your TikTok account.
- **Cross-Promote on Your Website or Blog**: Use your website or blog to drive traffic to your TikTok account by embedding your TikTok videos or adding social media buttons that lead to your profile. You can also create blog posts or pages that discuss TikTok trends or provide tutorials related to your niche, linking back to your TikTok.
- **Build an Email List**: Encourage followers to join your email list to receive updates, discounts, or exclusive content. Use TikTok videos to promote your email sign-up form and integrate your TikTok profile link in email newsletters.
- **Collaborate Across Platforms**: Collaborate with influencers or creators on other platforms. This can help you tap into their audience and drive them to your TikTok.

Paid promotions and cross-platform strategies allow you to scale your efforts and reach new audiences more effectively, accelerating your growth. As you grow, continue to monitor analytics to fine-tune your approach and maximize your results.

IDEA 8: Overcoming Common Challenges

Dealing with Creative Blocks

Creative blocks are a natural part of the content creation process. Every creator faces moments where inspiration seems to disappear. Here's how to push through those tough times:

- **Take a Break**: Sometimes, the best way to overcome a creative block is to step away. Take time off from creating and engage with other content to refresh your mind.
- **Brainstorm and Experiment**: Create a list of potential content ideas, even if they seem far-fetched. Experiment with different types of videos to see what resonates—whether it's new trends, collaborations, or personal stories.
- **Revisit Successful Content**: Look at your top-performing videos for inspiration. Try to understand what worked and build on those successful elements in new ways.
- **Get Feedback from Your Community**: Engage with your followers and ask them

what type of content they'd like to see. This not only helps overcome a creative block but also strengthens the bond with your audience.

- **Collaborate with Others**: Working with other creators can spark new ideas and bring a fresh perspective. A collaboration could lead to an unexpected creative breakthrough.

Managing Negativity and Online Trolls

While TikTok is a great platform for creativity, it can also expose creators to negativity and online trolls. Here's how to handle them:

- **Don't Take It Personally**: Remember that online trolls often seek to provoke a reaction. Keep your focus on your audience and your content goals.
- **Block or Report**: Don't hesitate to block or report users who are spreading hate, harassment, or inappropriate comments. TikTok's reporting system can help maintain a positive environment.
- **Stay Professional**: If you feel the need to respond to criticism, keep it respectful and professional. Negative comments can be an opportunity for growth if handled constructively.
- **Engage with Positive Comments**: Encourage positive conversations by responding to kind comments and fostering a supportive environment in your community.

- **Mental Health Check**: It's important to protect your mental health. If negativity becomes overwhelming, take a break or limit your social media exposure. Prioritize your well-being over online drama.

Staying Updated with Platform Changes

TikTok is constantly evolving, with new features, trends, and algorithm updates shaping the platform. To stay ahead, follow these tips:

- **Follow TikTok's Official Channels**: TikTok's Creator Portal, blog, and social media accounts provide updates on new features, changes to the algorithm, and best practices.
- **Join Creator Communities**: Engage with other TikTok creators through forums, social media groups, and online communities. They often share insights, tips, and news about changes to the platform.
- **Test New Features Early**: When TikTok introduces new features or tools, try them out early to see how they impact your content and engagement. Experimenting with new features can help you stand out.
- **Adapt Your Content Strategy**: Keep an eye on new trends, features, and algorithm changes. Be ready to adapt your content strategy to take advantage of new opportunities that may arise.
- **Learn from Analytics**: Consistently track the performance of your videos. If you

notice a drop or change in engagement, research possible updates or shifts in the TikTok platform that might be influencing your audience behavior.

By proactively addressing creative blocks, managing negativity, and staying informed about platform updates, you'll be better equipped to overcome common challenges on TikTok and continue growing your presence.

IDEA9: Case Studies

Success Stories of Creators and Brands

Examining the journeys of successful TikTok creators and brands can provide valuable insights into what makes content resonate with audiences. Here are a few examples of creators and brands who've excelled on TikTok:

1. Creator: Charli D'Amelio

Charli D'Amelio's rise to TikTok stardom is one of the most iconic success stories on the platform.

- **Niche**: Dance routines and challenges.
- **Growth**: Charli went from an unknown teen to one of TikTok's most-followed creators in just a few months.
- **Key to Success**: Her ability to participate in viral challenges, create her own signature

dance moves, and consistently post high-quality content with a relatable, down-to-earth persona. Charli built a community by staying authentic and engaging with her fans through comments and responses.

2. Creator: Zach King

Zach King's "magic vines" and creative visual effects have earned him a massive following on TikTok.

- **Niche**: Visual illusions, magic tricks, and short-form storytelling.
- **Growth**: Zach King has been a content creator for years, but TikTok's format allowed him to break through with his creative and engaging videos that blur the line between reality and illusion.
- **Key to Success**: His mastery of editing, storytelling, and his ability to constantly surprise his audience. He's known for his clean, seamless tricks that leave viewers amazed and eager for more.

3. Brand: Gymshark

Gymshark is an example of a brand that has used TikTok to amplify its reach and connect with younger audiences.

- **Niche**: Fitness apparel and activewear.
- **Growth**: By partnering with fitness influencers, Gymshark was able to

establish a solid presence in the fitness community on TikTok.

- **Key to Success**: Their viral success lies in their strategy of using influencers to create authentic, lifestyle-driven content. Gymshark didn't rely solely on traditional advertisements but rather on organic brand partnerships and user-generated content. Their challenges, collaborations, and giveaways kept their audience engaged and loyal.

Analyzing Viral Content: What Made It Work?

Understanding what makes content go viral on TikTok is crucial for creators aiming to increase their reach. Let's break down some key elements of viral TikTok content:

1. Timing and Trends

- **Example**: The "Savage Love" dance challenge.
- **What Made It Work**: The viral dance challenge tied to a catchy song created momentum as more users participated. Creators who jumped on the trend early gained the most exposure.
- **Key Takeaway**: Viral content often aligns with trends, but being one of the first to participate in a trend or creating a unique twist can give you an edge.

2. Strong Hook in the First Few Seconds

- **Example**: "The Magic Vine" videos by Zach King.
- **What Made It Work**: Zach King's videos immediately grabbed attention with their mystery and intrigue. The first few seconds built suspense and made viewers want to keep watching to see how the trick was done.
- **Key Takeaway**: Successful TikTok videos often have a strong hook in the first 2-3 seconds, whether it's an intriguing visual, a challenge, or an unexpected twist.

3. Relatable and Authentic Content

- **Example**: Charli D'Amelio's casual dance videos.
- **What Made It Work**: Charli's content was highly relatable, especially for teens. Her approachable personality and simple dance routines connected with a wide audience.
- **Key Takeaway**: Audiences gravitate towards creators who appear genuine and relatable. Authenticity in content fosters stronger connections with viewers, which drives engagement.

4. Engagement and Interactivity

- **Example**: "Flip the Switch" challenge.
- **What Made It Work**: This challenge encouraged people to participate, often in a humorous or unexpected way, which encouraged more engagement and sparked creativity.

- **Key Takeaway**: Content that encourages user interaction—whether through challenges, duet participation, or responding to comments—tends to spread rapidly across the platform.

5. Storytelling and Emotional Connection

- **Example**: Viral skits or story-based content (e.g., relatable parent-child interactions, funny work scenarios).
- **What Made It Work**: Content that tells a compelling story or evokes an emotional response tends to stick with viewers. Whether it's humor, inspiration, or vulnerability, emotions play a significant role in sharing content.
- **Key Takeaway**: Emotional storytelling in short-form videos creates a lasting impression, prompting viewers to share and engage.

Key Takeaways for Content Creators

From these case studies and content breakdowns, here are the essential factors that drive viral TikTok content:

- **Stay on top of trends**, but put your own spin on them.
- **Engage early with new trends** for better chances of virality.
- **Create a strong hook** within the first few seconds.

- **Maintain authenticity** and stay true to your unique style.
- **Incorporate storytelling** or emotions to make your content memorable.
- **Encourage audience participation** through challenges, duets, and interactive content.

By analyzing these success stories and content strategies, creators and brands can better understand how to craft videos that resonate with TikTok's community, increase engagement, and set the stage for viral success.

IDEA10: The Future of TikTok and Short Videos

Emerging Trends in Short-Form Content

As TikTok continues to lead the short-video trend, several emerging patterns point to the future direction of this content format. These trends highlight how TikTok and other platforms may evolve, offering new opportunities for creators and brands alike.

1. Vertical Video and Enhanced Immersion

- **Trend**: Vertical video format has become the norm across multiple social platforms, and its dominance will continue as mobile-first experiences remain at the forefront of digital engagement. Expect to see more

immersive features such as 3D or AR integrations within vertical video formats.
- **Impact**: Content that blends immersive technology like augmented reality (AR) or interactive elements will increase viewer engagement by offering more dynamic experiences. Expect TikTok to introduce more in-app effects and filters that can seamlessly integrate with live videos and stories.

2. Increased Integration of E-Commerce

- **Trend**: Social commerce is growing rapidly, and platforms like TikTok are increasing their focus on e-commerce capabilities, making it easier for creators to sell products directly from videos.
- **Impact**: Expect a shift toward more interactive, shoppable video content, where brands and creators alike will leverage TikTok's tools for direct sales. Livestream shopping, product tagging, and integrations with e-commerce platforms like Shopify will become more mainstream.

3. AI-Powered Personalization

- **Trend**: TikTok's algorithm is already powered by AI, but future iterations will see even more refined and personalized content recommendations. AI will be used to not only curate videos based on user preferences but also generate content for creators using AI-assisted tools.

- **Impact**: As AI continues to advance, creators will have access to new tools for video editing, content creation, and even voiceovers. Personalized AI suggestions will help creators hone their content for specific audiences with more precision than ever before.

4. Longer Short-Form Videos

- **Trend**: While TikTok started with a strict 15-second limit, they have since expanded to allow videos up to 10 minutes. We may see more emphasis on longer short-form videos that balance the need for quick, snackable content with deeper storytelling.
- **Impact**: Creators may explore hybrid content formats, using longer videos to go in-depth on topics while maintaining a fast-paced and engaging structure. Content such as mini-documentaries, tutorials, and short films could become more common, catering to an audience that craves more substantial content but within the framework of short-form video.

5. The Rise of Niche Communities and Micro-Creators

- **Trend**: As TikTok's algorithm becomes more precise, the platform will see the rise of hyper-targeted niche communities, leading to more personalized content experiences. Micro-creators who produce highly specialized content for specific audiences will thrive.

- **Impact**: The next wave of TikTok creators will focus on highly specific topics or interests, gaining loyal followings within niche communities. These creators will be able to drive deep engagement with their audiences, and brands may shift towards working with micro-influencers for more authentic, grassroots marketing.

Adapting to Evolving Audience Preferences

As TikTok evolves, so do the expectations and preferences of its audience. Staying ahead of these shifts will require creators to remain adaptable and responsive to changing behaviors.

1. The Shift to Authentic and Transparent Content

- **Trend**: TikTok users, especially Gen Z, have shown a preference for more authentic, unfiltered content. This preference is likely to continue as users demand more transparency from creators and brands.
- **Impact**: Creators who engage in "real" content that showcases vulnerabilities, behind-the-scenes moments, or genuine personal stories will continue to build strong relationships with their audiences. Audiences are moving away from polished, heavily edited content and gravitating toward "raw" content that feels real and unvarnished.

2. Increasing Demand for Educational Content

- **Trend**: While TikTok is often associated with entertainment and viral trends, the platform has seen a rise in educational content—spanning topics like finance, health, and personal development.
- **Impact**: Creators who can provide valuable, easy-to-digest knowledge in a quick, engaging format will see continued success. With TikTok's algorithm prioritizing content that keeps users engaged, educational content that also entertains or informs will be in demand.

3. Emphasis on Mental Health and Social Awareness

- **Trend**: Social movements and mental health awareness have been gaining more attention on social platforms. TikTok has increasingly become a place for users to express their concerns, share stories, and raise awareness about important issues.
- **Impact**: Content related to social causes, mental health, and personal well-being will likely continue to resonate with TikTok's audience. Creators who align with social movements or produce content that advocates for positive change will strengthen their community ties and boost engagement.

Preparing for the Next Big Platform Shift

The world of social media is constantly changing, and staying ahead of the curve is essential for continued success. TikTok, as the current frontrunner in short-form video content, will undoubtedly face competition from new platforms, while also adapting to challenges and innovations in the tech space.

1. Embrace Multiplatform Strategies

- **Future Shift**: As TikTok faces more competition, such as from Instagram Reels or YouTube Shorts, creators will need to expand their presence beyond one platform.
- **Preparation**: Building a brand presence across multiple social media platforms will be essential to mitigating risk and reaching a broader audience. Leveraging TikTok's strengths while diversifying content across Instagram, YouTube, and other platforms can help creators adapt to shifting trends.

2. Innovative Technologies

- **Future Shift**: Emerging technologies, like 5G, AR, and VR, will offer new ways to engage with short-form content. TikTok may integrate more of these technologies to keep the platform fresh and interactive.
- **Preparation**: Creators will need to learn how to use these new technologies, like

incorporating AR filters, VR experiences, or 360-degree videos, to stay relevant and ahead of the curve. Being open to experimenting with new tech will be key in maintaining engagement.

3. Audience Behavior and Evolving Content Consumption

- **Future Shift**: User behavior will continue to evolve as younger generations grow up with new social media platforms and experiences. Short-form content may become integrated into even more digital spaces, such as VR environments, live streaming, and interactive experiences.
- **Preparation**: Keep an eye on user behavior trends, including shifts in how long people spend on social media or what content types are emerging as most popular. Flexibility in adapting to these changes will help creators stay competitive.

Key Takeaways for Creators:

- Embrace the **evolution of short-form content**, including AR/VR, e-commerce integration, and hybrid video lengths.
- Stay adaptable to evolving **audience preferences**, especially for authenticity, educational content, and mental health discussions.

- Be ready to **diversify your presence across platforms** and **adopt new technologies** as they emerge.

By preparing for these shifts, creators can not only thrive in the current TikTok landscape but also remain ahead of the curve as the platform evolves and new opportunities arise.

Conclusion:

Recap of Key Strategies

As we reach the end of this guide, let's recap the key strategies that will set you on the path to success on TikTok:

1. **Understanding the Algorithm**: The power of TikTok lies in its algorithm. By focusing on watch time, engagement, and consistency, you can maximize your visibility on the "For You" page (FYP).
2. **Setting a Solid Foundation**: Start by defining your niche, understanding your audience, and optimizing your profile. Tools and apps for video editing are crucial for creating polished content.
3. **Crafting Irresistible Content**: The key to viral videos is in the hook, story, and call-to-action. Stay authentic, relatable, and creative, and use the platform's music, effects, and transitions effectively to stand out.

4. **Engaging with Your Audience**: Interact with your followers through comments, duets, and live sessions. Building a loyal community is essential for long-term success.
5. **Harnessing Trends, Hashtags, and Challenges**: Stay on top of trends, use relevant hashtags, and participate in challenges to increase discoverability and engagement.
6. **Monetizing Your TikTok**: Take advantage of TikTok's monetization features like the Creator Fund, collaborations, and direct sales through the platform.
7. **Analyzing Growth**: Use TikTok's analytics to understand your performance and adjust your strategies. Cross-platform promotion and paid ads can help scale your content.
8. **Overcoming Challenges**: Every creator faces obstacles—whether it's dealing with creative blocks, negative feedback, or changes in the platform. Stay adaptable, keep learning, and remain consistent.
9. **Looking to the Future**: TikTok's landscape is ever-changing. Stay ahead by embracing emerging trends, evolving with audience preferences, and exploring new technologies.

Inspiring the Reader to Take the First Step

Now that you've been equipped with the essential knowledge and strategies, it's time to take action. TikTok offers immense potential for creativity and growth, but it's up to you to make the first move.

Start by brainstorming your niche, experimenting with content, and engaging with your audience. Consistency and authenticity are the keys to success, so dive in with confidence, and remember that every small step brings you closer to your goals.

Whether you're aiming to build a brand, grow your personal following, or monetize your content, TikTok is a tool that can unlock endless possibilities. The best time to start is now. Your journey as a TikTok creator awaits!

Final Thoughts: TikTok as a Tool for Creativity and Growth

TikTok is not just a platform for entertainment—it's a powerful tool for self-expression, community-building, and entrepreneurship. With its ever-evolving features, TikTok offers endless opportunities for creative individuals to showcase their talents, connect with like-minded people, and even build businesses.

As a creator, you have the power to shape the narrative, challenge norms, and engage with a global audience. TikTok is a dynamic and vibrant space where innovation thrives. Whether you're sharing a quick dance routine or offering valuable insights, remember that creativity has no limits on TikTok.

Take the leap, trust the process, and use TikTok to unlock your potential. The future is yours to create!

Additional Resources: TikTok Editing Tools and Apps

To help you create high-quality, engaging TikTok content, here are some essential editing tools and apps that can enhance your videos and streamline your creative process:

1. InShot

- **Features**: InShot is a popular video editor with easy-to-use features like trimming, speed adjustments, filters, effects, and music integration. It also offers a range of templates and allows you to add text, stickers, and transitions.
- **Why it's useful**: Perfect for beginners and experienced creators alike, InShot helps you create polished, professional-looking videos quickly.
- **Platform**: Available on iOS and Android.

2. CapCut

- **Features**: CapCut is a free, feature-rich video editing app created by ByteDance (the parent company of TikTok). It includes advanced features like chroma key (green screen), transitions, effects, and automatic captions.
- **Why it's useful**: As a TikTok partner app, CapCut provides seamless integration with

the platform, making it easy to upload your content.

- **Platform**: Available on iOS and Android.

3. Adobe Premiere Rush

- **Features**: Adobe Premiere Rush offers powerful video editing capabilities in a user-friendly interface. It allows you to trim, add text, apply transitions, and adjust audio levels.
- **Why it's useful**: If you're looking for a more professional editing tool that's still easy to use, Premiere Rush is a great choice.
- **Platform**: Available on iOS, Android, and desktop.

4. Kinemaster

- **Features**: Kinemaster offers a full suite of editing tools, including multi-layer video editing, transitions, effects, speed controls, and audio mixing.
- **Why it's useful**: It's perfect for creators who want to take their editing to the next level with more precise controls.
- **Platform**: Available on iOS and Android.

5. Videoleap

- **Features**: Videoleap is an intuitive video editing app that offers creative tools such as multi-layer editing, motion graphics, keyframes, and a variety of special effects.

- **Why it's useful**: Ideal for those who want to add more advanced, cinematic touches to their TikTok videos.
- **Platform**: Available on iOS.

6. TikTok's Built-In Editor

- **Features**: TikTok's native video editor offers various features like trimming, adding effects, filters, transitions, text overlays, stickers, and music directly within the app.
- **Why it's useful**: For creators who want to quickly create content without needing external apps, TikTok's built-in editor is a simple and efficient tool.
- **Platform**: Available directly within the TikTok app.

7. iMovie

- **Features**: iMovie is a great entry-level video editing app, offering features like cutting, trimming, and adding text and music. It's known for its clean interface and ease of use.
- **Why it's useful**: Perfect for quick edits on Apple devices with basic editing needs.
- **Platform**: Available on iOS and macOS.

8. Veed.io

- **Features**: Veed.io is an online editing tool that allows you to add subtitles, filters, and transitions to videos. It also offers an easy drag-and-drop interface for fast editing.

- **Why it's useful**: If you prefer working on your desktop or laptop, Veed.io offers a simple, web-based solution for editing and exporting TikTok videos.
- **Platform**: Web-based, no download needed.

9. FilmoraGo

- **Features**: FilmoraGo offers a full suite of video editing features, including reverse playback, slow motion, trimming, and visual effects. It also provides templates and an easy-to-use interface.
- **Why it's useful**: Ideal for beginners and intermediate creators who want professional-looking videos without needing to master complex editing software.
- **Platform**: Available on iOS and Android.

10. Canva

- **Features**: While Canva is known for graphic design, it also offers simple video editing features, including templates, transitions, text animations, and music options.
- **Why it's useful**: Great for adding branded elements, such as intros, outros, and titles, as well as for creating eye-catching thumbnails.
- **Platform**: Web-based and available on iOS and Android.

Tips for Using Editing Tools Effectively:

- **Consistency**: Use similar editing styles for your videos to establish a recognizable brand. Whether it's using the same color palette, text style, or effects, consistency builds familiarity.
- **Timing**: The timing of cuts, transitions, and music is crucial to keeping your videos engaging. Aim for smooth edits that enhance the flow without making it feel rushed.
- **Experiment**: Don't be afraid to experiment with different editing styles and tools. Over time, you'll find what works best for your audience and your personal style.

By utilizing these tools, you'll be able to create high-quality TikTok content that stands out and engages your audience.

Would you like any specific advice on using any of these apps or tools for particular types of content?

Content Calendars and Planning Templates

A content calendar is an essential tool for organizing your TikTok strategy and ensuring consistency in your posting. Here are some helpful templates and tips to help you plan and schedule your content effectively.

1. Monthly Content Calendar Template

A monthly calendar allows you to plan your content in advance, ensuring a balanced mix of videos that align with your niche and audience. Here's a simple structure to follow:

Date	Content Idea	Type of Content	Hashtags	Call to Action	Notes
January 1	New Year's Resol	Motivational/ Inspirational	#NewYears Resolutions #2025	Foll ow for mor	Focu s on trend ing resol

Date	Content Idea	Type of Content	Hashtags	Call to Action	
	ution Ideas			e tips	ution s
January 4	Behind-the-scenes of my daily routine	Vlog/Personal	#BehindTheScenes #Routine	What's your routine?	Share in a relatable way
January 7	TikTok Growth Tips	Educational	#TikTokTips #GrowthHacks	Save and share with friends	Include actionable advice
January 10	Trending dance challenge	Fun/Challenge	#TrendingDance #Challenge	Try this with your friends	Use popular music

How to Use It:

- **Content Idea**: Briefly describe what type of content you plan to create.
- **Type of Content**: Identify whether it's a tutorial, challenge, personal story, etc.
- **Hashtags**: Use trending and niche hashtags relevant to the content.
- **Call to Action**: A prompt to engage your audience (e.g., "Follow", "Share", "Comment").

- **Notes**: Special notes about your content, such as adding effects or music, or any specific promotion.

2. Weekly Content Planner

A weekly content planner focuses on more immediate details, helping you organize your videos by the day of the week and track performance.

Day	Content Title	Platform /Format	Goal/Objective	Performance Metrics	Engagement Actions
Monday	Start Your Week with a Positive Tip	TikTok Video	Increase engagement	Likes, shares, comments	Reply to all comments
Tuesday	Trending Recipe Tutorial	TikTok Video	Build follower base	Watch time, saves	Ask followers for feedback
Wednesday	Q&A: Answering Your Questions	TikTok Live	Boost interaction rate	Views, viewer count	Interact with viewers live
Thursday	Behind-the-Scenes Vlog	TikTok Video	Personal connection	Comments, likes	Ask followers for suggestions
Friday	Trend Participation	TikTok Video	Trend engagement	Shares, comme	Use popula

			nts, followers	r music

How to Use It:

- **Content Title**: Give a short title to the video or content piece.
- **Platform/Format**: Specify if it's a TikTok video, live session, or other.
- **Goal/Objective**: What do you want to achieve with the video (e.g., engagement, visibility)?
- **Performance Metrics**: Track important metrics like views, likes, shares, and comments to measure success.
- **Engagement Actions**: Focus on activities like commenting back, collaborating with others, or using specific hashtags to boost interaction.

3. Content Theme and Format Ideas Template

This template helps you brainstorm and structure your content into various themes and formats, allowing you to stay organized and focused.

Theme	Video Format	Content Ideas	Frequency	Notes
Educational Content	Tutorials, Tips, How-Tos	TikTok growth tips, Life hacks, Niche advice	2-3 times a week	Always provide value

Personal Content	Vlogs, Behind-the-scenes	Day-in-the-life, Personal stories, Routines	1-2 times a week	Connect with audience
Challenges & Trends	Trend participation, Duets	Participate in trending challenges, dance videos	1-2 times a week	Follow TikTok trends closely
Motivational/Inspiration	Short Clips, Quotes	Motivational tips, Positive affirmations	1-2 times a week	Stay uplifting and positive
Product Reviews	Unboxing, Demos	Review new products, Services you use	1 time a week	Promote affiliate links

How to Use It:

- **Theme**: Organize content by its core message (education, personal, trends, etc.).
- **Video Format**: Identify whether it's a vlog, tutorial, or challenge video.
- **Content Ideas**: Jot down specific video ideas under each theme.
- **Frequency**: Set a goal for how often to post under each theme.
- **Notes**: Keep any additional ideas or reminders for each type of content.

4. Daily Task Checklist

A daily checklist helps you stay organized with the repetitive tasks that support your content creation process. Here's a sample template:

Task	Completed (✓)
Check TikTok trends and hashtags	
Review and reply to comments	
Record/edit/upload new video	
Engage with followers (like, comment)	
Monitor analytics (views, engagement)	
Plan next content piece	

How to Use It:

- Break down your daily content creation process into manageable tasks.
- Check off tasks as you complete them to stay on track.

Tips for Effective Content Planning:

- **Batch Content Creation**: Plan and create multiple videos in one go to stay ahead of schedule.
- **Track Trends**: Keep an eye on what's trending within your niche or globally to remain relevant.

- **Consistency is Key**: Stick to your posting schedule and be consistent with your engagement to build trust with your audience.
- **Repurpose Content**: Don't be afraid to repurpose successful content across different formats, like turning a video into a still image or turning a live session into short clips.

TikTok Creators and Accounts to Follow for Inspiration

1. Creative/Editing Mastery:

- **@itsjojosiwa** – JoJo Siwa's account showcases bright, high-energy content with impeccable editing and transitions.
- **@maxsommerfeld** – A creator who blends visually stunning edits with a lot of fun and creative effects.
- **@thejazminshow** – Features creative and clever transitions that grab attention, and focuses on fun, fast-paced edits.

2. Educational Content:

- **@chemistryteacherphil** – A science educator who explains concepts in a creative, engaging way using simple experiments.
- **@danielsinclair** – A tech educator sharing quick tips, hacks, and knowledge about

digital tools, often in a bite-sized and entertaining format.

- **@dailydoseofhistory** – History enthusiasts will find this account educational and fascinating, as it delivers historical tidbits in a short, engaging style.

3. Business & Marketing:

- **@garyvee** – Gary Vaynerchuk shares his business wisdom, motivational insights, and tips on social media marketing.
- **@mattdiavella** – A creator focused on minimalism, productivity, and self-improvement, offering tips to improve life and work.
- **@alexisfrazier** – Social media strategist sharing tips on how to grow and optimize your online presence, especially on TikTok.

4. Humor & Comedy:

- **@charlidamelio** – Charli D'Amelio is not only famous for dancing but also for adding humor and relatability to her content.
- **@kingbach** – Comedian and actor who frequently shares funny skits and viral challenges with a fast-paced, engaging style.

- **@daviddobrik** – Known for comedic vlogs and high-energy humor, David shares both scripted and spontaneous fun content.

5. Fitness and Motivation:

- **@emilyskyefit** – A fitness creator who shares workout routines, tips, and motivational content for a healthy lifestyle.
- **@chrisheria** – Focuses on calisthenics, offering workout tips and motivation for fitness enthusiasts.
- **@thebetternotbitterproject** – A body positivity account that promotes fitness while focusing on mental health and self-love.

6. Fashion and Style:

- **@lindseystern** – Known for her fashion-forward content, Lindsey offers styling tips, sustainable fashion choices, and confidence-building tips.
- **@brittanyxavier** – Fashion influencer sharing her daily outfits, styling tricks, and tips on how to create fashionable looks on a budget.
- **@patriciamanfield** – Shares minimalist and chic fashion ideas, with a special focus on how to mix and match clothes.

7. DIY & Crafts:

- **@crafty.diy.er** – A DIY creator showing step-by-step tutorials on how to create unique home decor and craft projects.
- **@therealalishablack** – Known for her simple yet creative DIY home improvement ideas and crafts.
- **@diydave** – Offers fun, creative ways to make inexpensive DIY projects for home decor, gifts, and fashion.

8. Food & Cooking:

- **@thekitchenwhisperer** – Shares simple yet delicious recipes, cooking tips, and food hacks.
- **@amberbaker** – Focuses on easy-to-make recipes and offers tips on cooking from scratch, with an emphasis on healthy meals.
- **@chefmarcusb** – Offers both professional tips for cooking as well as lighthearted, funny food-related content.

9. Travel & Adventure:

- **@jacksonheath** – A travel vlogger who shares his adventures in breathtaking locations around the world, combined with travel tips and hacks.
- **@sophiegama** – A globetrotter who shows her adventures across different countries, with great video editing and travel hacks.
- **@thejourneyofjess** – Offers a mix of travel inspiration, destination highlights, and tips on how to explore on a budget.

10. Personal Development & Life Advice:

- **@the.bestself** – Focuses on self-improvement, productivity, and mental health, offering tips to help you live your best life.
- **@themindsetmentor** – Shares motivational content to inspire others to build a positive mindset and achieve personal goals.
- **@therealjessicajames** – A motivational speaker who shares lessons on overcoming challenges, self-worth, and resilience.

11. Tech and Gadgets:

- **@techgeekbrian** – Offers tech reviews, tutorials, and guides on the latest gadgets and tech news.
- **@imranpatel** – Known for his deep dives into the latest technological trends and gadget reviews, including TikTok tips.
- **@codingwithchris** – Shares coding tutorials and tech tips for anyone interested in learning programming and software development.

These accounts can inspire you with various styles, from creative editing and trending challenges to educational content and business strategies. Make sure to observe the different types of engagement techniques they use and think about how you can apply similar strategies to your own content.

If you need more specific recommendations based on your niche, feel free to ask!

www.ingramcontent.com/pod-product-compliance
Lightning Source LLC
LaVergne TN
LVHW052315060326
832902LV00021B/3906